dora the donkey

by Gisela Buck and Siegfried Buck

GF

For a free color catalog describing Gareth Stevens Publishing's list of high-quality books and multimedia programs, call 1-800-542-2595 (USA) or 1-800-461-9120 (Canada). Gareth Stevens Publishing's Fax: (414) 225-0377. See our catalog, too, on the World Wide Web: http://gsinc.com

Library of Congress Cataloging-in-Publication Data available upon request from publisher. Fax: (414) 225-0377 for the attention of the Publishing Records Department.

ISBN 0-8368-1505-X

First published in North America in 1997 by
Gareth Stevens Publishing
1555 North RiverCenter Drive, Suite 201
Milwaukee, Wisconsin 53212 USA

This edition first published in 1997 by Gareth Stevens, Inc. Original edition © 1993 by Kinderbuchverlag KBV Luzern, Sauerländer AG, Aarau, Switzerland, under the title *Mona, das Eselfohlen*. Translated from the German by John E. Hayes. Adapted by Gareth Stevens, Inc. All additional material supplied for this edition © 1997 by Gareth Stevens, Inc.

Photographer: Andreas Fischer-Nagel, except pp. 8-9, 10-11 by Dorothy Morris
Watercolor artist: Wolfgang Kill
Series editors: Barbara J. Behm and Patricia Lantier-Sampon
Editorial assistants: Diane Laska, Jamie Daniel, and Rita Reitci

Printed in Mexico
1 2 3 4 5 6 7 8 9 01 00 99 98 97

J636.1
BUC

Gareth Stevens Publishing
MILWAUKEE

Have you ever seen a donkey
at the zoo or on a farm?

Donkeys have long
ears and soft, curly
coats. A male
donkey is called
a stallion.

A female donkey is a mare.
This stallion and mare will
soon be parents.

The mare will give birth to a baby donkey,
or foal. For now, she rests in the soft hay.

The foal grows inside its
mother's body.

After the mare has carried her foal for twelve months, she gives birth.

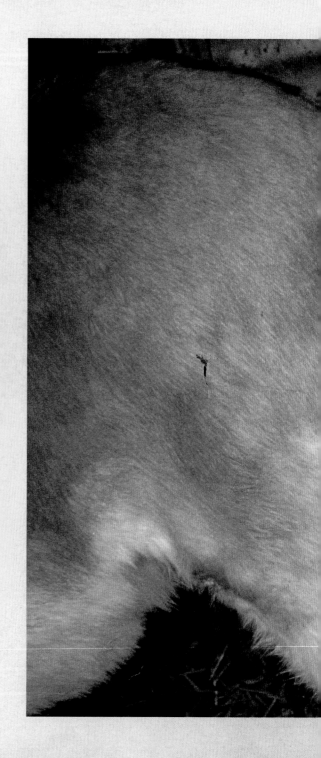

The foal makes its way
out of its mother's body
to begin a life of its own.

The newborn donkey
is named Dora.

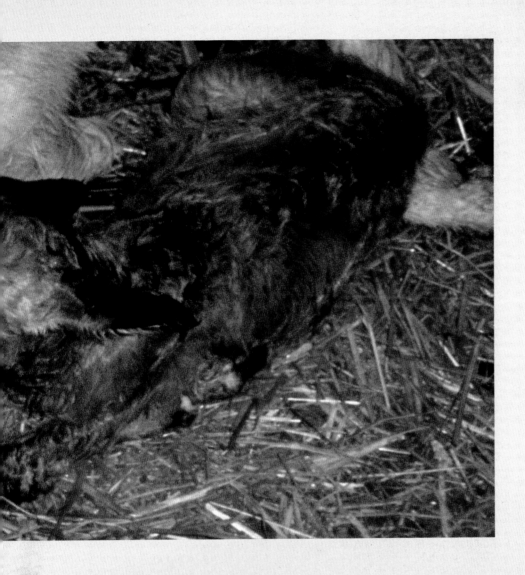

She is a mare.

The mother licks Dora's
coat clean.

Dora begins to sniff around. She sniffs
her mother and will always know her
mother by this scent, or smell.

Just fifteen minutes
after being born, Dora
stands up.

She is hungry and wants to
nurse, or drink milk from
her mother's body.

This milk will help Dora
grow big and strong.

Two hours after being born,
Dora walks.

Dora's father sniffs his newborn foal.
He makes the sound of "Hee-haw,
hee-haw, hee-haw!"

Dora has found a new friend, Anna.
Anna is strong and can lift the
30-pound (14-kilogram) donkey.

Dora plays in the meadow.
She likes to run through the
soft, green grass.

Dora is tired after a busy
day in the meadow.

But soon she is up
playing again.

Dora needs to run and
play to stay healthy.

She always has fun with
the family dog.

When Dora is three days old,
she begins to eat grass. She will
still drink her mother's milk, too,
for six more months.

Every day, Dora's mother licks her foal clean from head to tail.

From her mother, Dora learns to roll in the dirt. This protects donkeys from flies and fleas.

Dora is an adult at
one year old.

When she is three years old, she
can become a mother, too.

Further Reading and Videos

At the Zoo. (Learning Videos)

Baby Animals. (Film Ideas, Inc.)

Caballos, Caballos, Caballos: Horses, Horses, Horses. Fowler (Childrens Press) (bilingual, Spanish/English)

Debra the Donkey. Hammond (Warner)

The Donkey on the Bridge. Jafa (Children's Book Trust)

Farm Animals. Animals at a Glance (series). Isabella Dudek (Gareth Stevens)

For the Love of Animals: Farm Animals. (GCG Productions video)

Horses. Animal Families (series). Hans D. Dossenbach (Gareth Stevens)

A Visit to the Farm. (New World Video)

Wonders of Donkeys. Lavine and Scaro (Putnam)

Fun Facts about Donkeys

Did you know . . .

— that the offspring of a female horse and a male donkey is called a mule? Mules cannot produce their own offspring.

— that donkeys are 3-5 feet (1-1.5 meters) tall?

— that donkeys were first tamed by humans about five thousand years ago?

— that donkeys eat foods like thistles and thorn bushes that few other animals can eat?

Glossary-Index

adult — fully developed or mature; grown-up (p. 22).

birth — the act of being born or bearing young (pp. 4, 6).

coat — the outer covering, such as hair or fur, of an animal (pp. 2, 10).

fleas — tiny insects that bite animals, including humans, and drink their blood (p. 21).

flies — winged insects that have thin, clear wings (p. 21).

foal — a young horse, donkey, or zebra (pp. 4, 5, 6, 7, 15, 21).

hay — cut and sometimes dried grass, clover, and other plants. Hay is often used as food and bedding for various animals (p. 4).

kilogram — a basic unit of the metric system. One kilogram is equal to 2.205 pounds (p. 16).

mare — an adult female horse, donkey, or zebra (pp. 3, 4, 6, 9).

meadow — an area of moist, low-lying land with grasses on it (pp. 17, 18).

nurse — to drink the milk produced by a female mammal's body for nourishment (p. 12).

protect — to guard or keep safe from injury or harm (p. 21).

scent — a specific and particular smell (p. 10).

sniff — to smell or draw air up into the nose (pp. 10, 15).

stallion — an adult male horse, donkey, or zebra (pp. 2, 3).